101 TIPS FOR
CAREER SUCCESS

Ray Harrell, MS, MBA, SHRM-SCP

ISBN-13: 978-1484183069
ISBN-10: 1484183061

101 Tips for Career Success
© 2013, Ray Harrell
© 2017, WeStone Resource Management

Have you ever been rejected for a job and always wondered why you were not hired? Depending on how far along you were in the selection process, it could be any number of factors. Most reputable organizations truly select candidates based on their qualifications, education, experience, and credentials. However, there are some employers whose selection methods are dubious at best!

Regardless that your rejection letter may state that they selected "a candidate whose qualifications more closely matched the needs of the position," there are often underlying reasons why job seekers are not selected. To avoid litigation and Equal Employment Opportunity Commission (EEOC) charges, organizations have crafted unique and ambiguous rejection letters.

If you have gotten one or more of these letters, do not give up hope. Take a step back, take a moment to breathe, and use the job search, résumé, and interview tips in this book to refocus your job search. Ironically, there is something even more discouraging and frustrating than getting scores of rejection letters. Not receiving any communication at all from an employer to which someone has applied often leaves job seekers in a state of uncertainty. Such lack of communication about the status of the position, especially after a candidate has taken the time to go in for an in-person interview, shows a complete lack of regard and professionalism, and quite honestly, is a direct reflection of the organization's culture!

Embarking on the hunt for a job can be a very frustrating, but necessary, evil. In this employer's market, job seekers must create for themselves an almost fairy-tale image in order to compete with the hundreds of people often competing for the same job!

There are hundreds of books and web sites out there that will give you a few tips on how to present yourself to a potential employer. Most of them are accurate; some of them are severely outdated. This book is designed to put a humorous twist to the otherwise irritating process of looking for a job. Based on combined years of experience reviewing résumés and interviewing candidates, along with information shared by colleagues, you can benefit from this resource full of current trends and increase your chances of landing that perfect job.

While this book does not provide any guarantee of a job offer, it includes valuable tips that every job seeker should follow. Some recruiter and hiring manager secrets are exposed to help you get past the roadblocks that may seem to hinder you from finding employment.

The tips in this book are organized in such a way that they usher you from the beginning of your job search all the way through to your final interview and acceptance of an offer.

Best of luck. Enjoy!

Tip #1
'Tis The Season!

What season is it? Job hunting season! If you are not currently employed, but you would like to be, then looking for employment has now become your full time job! Losing a job is not an opportunity for you to relax and take it easy. Even if you are currently receiving unemployment compensation, or have received some sort of severance package from your previous employer, it is not a good idea to allow yourself to become complacent or lackadaisical.

The longer you are out of work, the harder it will be to become employed, especially if you aren't occupying your time with something productive, measurable and transferrable. Additionally, the longer you are out of the workforce, the less prepared you will be should you manage to score a job interview. You will gradually fall out of the practice of speaking the industry jargon that you have become accustomed to in previous positions.

You should expect to spend at least 4 hours every weekday on tasks related to your job search, including completing applications, interviewing, and researching companies. You should also spend time practicing interview question responses, perfecting your answers, and refining your speech patterns (See Tip #76). Treat each day as if you were reporting to a job. Wake up early, get dressed, and pour yourself a cup of coffee. Dedicate a space in your home (or library, or coffee shop) where you can be away from distractions and concentrate fully on your job search.

Tip #2
Testing, Testing, 1, 2, 3!

Many organizations, especially companies where worker safety is of major concern (manufacturing, construction, and other positions working with heavy equipment, machinery, or transportation), will require pre-employment and ongoing random drug testing. To increase your chances of gaining and keeping employment, assuming you are a partaker, now would be a good time to consider giving up illicit drugs.

Organizations with a well-designed and administered random drug testing program will eventually weed out illicit drug users, in spite of any pills, liquids, or devices commonly used to circumvent the system.

In most cases, there is a legitimate business reason, such as safety, for monitoring and testing employees for drug use. It's not that employers want to control your life outside of work, but they want to make sure that you are sober and alert on the job and are physically and mentally able to perform your duties in a safe and productive manner.

Tip #3
Paper Or Plastic?

Almost all employers are now using some sort of electronic applicant tracking system (ATS) or search system to recruit applicants (See Tip #37). Long gone are the days of walking into an establishment's "personnel office" and asking for a paper application, filling it out, and getting an on-the-spot interview.

Technology has allowed the entire recruiting process, from the job posting to on-boarding, to be streamlined and efficient.

If you are new to the job market, or are re-entering the job market for the first time in 15 years or so, make sure you have access to a computer with a reasonably fast internet connection, and make sure you have a professional email account (See Tips #8 & 9).

This is necessary because most ATSs require high internet bandwidth to process your application. The last thing you want is for your application to time-out after you have spent valuable time filling out the form.

Tip #4
Get To Work!

Before you begin your job search, create a "working résumé". Your working résumé will serve as your official, personal resource for all your employment information. It should contain your entire work history, even that job you held in high school or that volunteer position you held last summer. For each position include company names, addresses, phone numbers, supervisor names and contact information, job titles, the complete list of job duties, tasks, responsibilities, accomplishments, dates of employment (month and year), reasons for leaving, and your salary history with each organization.

Unlike your "professional résumé" (See Tip #5), this version may span 3 or 4 pages, or maybe even 10 pages. There is no page limit with your working résumé, as you are the only person who will have access to it.

Tip #5
Be Prepared!

The professional résumé is the formatted and visually appealing version that you give to potential employers, either during your interview, or that you send via postal mail, email, or online. It should be a summary of your relevant positions (only for the last 8-10 years or your last 3-4 positions), your major job duties and accomplishments, dates of employment, academic and professional credentials, and your contact information. Nothing more.

Be selective when choosing entries on your professional résumé. Don't over-do it. Your résumé is not a laundry list of everything you did at your previous employers, but a marketing piece to demonstrate how you solved a problem or added value at the various organizations during your career.

Tip #6
Does This Fit?

Unless you are only applying to one specific type of job, do not use one résumé for every job to which you are applying. Tailor it to fit each job application. Learn how to re-word your duties and accomplishments so they are relevant to the job. For example, if you were previously a file clerk and are applying for a call center position, you might say, "Provided efficient and courteous information retrieval services to internal customers." This will demonstrate that you have the ability to interface with people and provide requested information in a timely manner, which is a skill directly transferrable to a call center environment. Remember to always be honest when describing your duties. A good interviewer will be able to ask the right technical questions to determine whether or not you are being truthful.

Tip #7
Strike The Spare!

Unless directly relevant to the job for which you are applying, avoid listing anything that may reveal your ethnicity, religion, political views or social activity. This includes some volunteer activities, social affiliations, fraternities or sororities, student organizations and religious participation.

For example, let's say you included that you volunteered for the Worldwide Republican Convention, and your interviewer is a staunch, far-left Democrat; or say you indicate that you are a member of the Rifle Owner's Association, but your interviewer has consistently lobbied against gun ownership. While your activities and affiliations may be personally fulfilling and may add meaning to your life, insidious employers may use this information to eliminate you as a candidate.

Tip #8
It's A Date!

Believe it or not, some employers do still discriminate on the basis of age or perceived age. In fact, it's against the law to ask for a person's age or date of birth until after they accept a job offer (if the application does contain a date of birth field, leave it blank). Do not date yourself! Meaning do not reveal your age or give any indication of how old you might be on your résumé. Remove the year of your high school graduation unless that is the only educational experience you have, and it was relatively recent. Do not include jobs that are more than 10 years old. Also, check your email address to make sure it doesn't inadvertently reveal your age or the year you were born. For example, using an email address like email55@domain.com may cause interviewers to conclude that you were either born in 1955 or are 55 years old, both of which might result in age discrimination.

Tip #9
Don't Get Personal!

That funny, creative, and possibly vulgar email account you use to communicate with friends is not the one you should use for professional communications. No employer would take you seriously asking them to email you at juicybooty69@domain.com. If this is your only email account, it is imperative that you create a professional email account, ideally using some variation of your first and last name. Something similar to "john.smith@domain.com" would be most appropriate for job seekers.

Tip #10
Give Me My Ringback!

When you are applying for jobs, it is a great idea to modify your voicemail greeting. Make sure there are no ringback tones, slang, nicknames, profanity, music, or children in your voicemail greeting. An employer doesn't want to call your phone and listen to 15 seconds of music before you introduce yourself. Additionally, your selection of ringback tone might give a clue as to your possible ethnicity, age, or if nothing else, your interests. Make sure you are taken seriously about your job search.

A simple greeting indicating your name, and a message saying that you will return the call at your convenience is sufficient.

Tip #11
What's In A Name?

If your name is difficult to pronounce, or you are concerned it may reveal your ethnicity, consider using initials. For example, if your name is Iriquah Johnson, consider using "Ms. I. Johnson". Or if your name is Babatadunaunde Abooyegieha, use "B. Abooyegieha" or even consider using a pseudonym such as "B. Anderson". Be sure to use a handle (Mr. Ms. Mrs.) so the caller can ask for Ms. Johnson or Mr. Anderson.

After you secure the first interview, then you should reveal your true name. Some readers/reviewers may think this is dishonest, but if your name has been preventing you from getting interviews, this tactic just may change the game for you. Additionally, if you have a unisex name, or your name is one that has been traditionally assigned to the opposite sex, be sure to include a handle (ex: Mr. Beverly James).

Tip #12
Your Honor, I Object!

Objectives are a throwback to earlier times when there were more opportunities available than job seekers. The idea of the objective was to let the interviewer know what you were looking for in a career and how the organization could best meet your career goals.

In this market, employers do not care about what you want them to do for you; they want to know what you can do for them. If you must have something at the top of your résumé, include a one or two sentence "Professional Summary" or "Profile" describing what you can bring to the company. This is also known as your "Value Statement".

Avoid adopting over-used jargon and clichés like, "detail oriented" or "team player" in your profile. Break out that thesaurus and be creative. The idea is to stand out from the hundreds of other résumés submitted by job-seekers vying for the same position.

Tip #13
Me, Myself & I!

Avoid using personal pronouns on your résumé. Since your résumé is about **your** career accomplishments, **your** employment history, and **your** education, there is no need to re-identify yourself by using personal pronouns. For example, there is no need to say, "I successfully performed my duties in my position." Instead say, "Successfully performed the duties of the position."

Likewise, do not use second-person or third-person pronouns such as "their", "we", "our" to describe your employer, colleagues, or duties. It's not concise and makes your résumé more difficult to read.

Tip #14
Fluschnitzel Trabdiddies!

Avoid using company specific jargon, acronyms, and abbreviations. You may know what you are talking about, but the employer may not be familiar with your particular organization or industry. Instead of saying, "Cooked fluschnitzel trabdiddies every morning," say "Prepared 10,000 gourmet pastries before 7am daily." Bring up the fluschnitzel trabdiddies during your interview to make conversation and generate interest in your previous work.

Likewise, interviewers do not want to read, "Used FF to run the 9OD report for the DA during the GRB meetings." It's short and sweet, but when you spell it out so anyone can understand it translates to, "Used an industry standard accounting software to generate 90-day accounts receivable report for the Division Administrator to use during the General Regional Board meetings." Better yet, shorten that to say, "Used FiscalForce to generate past-due reports for regional leadership." This says the same thing and gives a plug for the type software you have used.

This will prove beneficial if the company for which you are applying happens to use the same software, or are familiar with the capabilities of the software. It will also ensure that your résumé is included in the results of a search on "FiscalForce".

Tip #15
Who's On First?

For each position you have listed on your professional résumé, make sure you list the most relevant accomplishment or job duty first. That will ensure that the employer will continue to read the rest of your résumé. The job description does not begin with "Other duties as assigned," so neither should your résumé.

If you begin your list of duties with something small and insignificant, say, "wiped off desk every night before going home," then that will appear to be the most important thing you did in your position, and there is really no reason to read further. Your first duty or accomplishment should grab the attention of the reader, such as, "Reduced costs by…", or "Improved customer retention by…". Seeing that first on the list will make the reader want to know how you accomplished those things, and what else you did to benefit your previous organization.

Tip #16
You Seem Tense!

Your current job accomplishments on your résumé should include present tense verbs, such as "Organize" or "Facilitate". All previous positions should use past-tense verbs, such as "Organized" and "Facilitated". Make sure there is subject/verb agreement throughout the body of your résumé.

Tip #17
Half Empty, Or Half Full?

Short on work experience? Use what you have! List the one job that you had and re-word it so your duties and accomplishments appear as relevant skills that are transferrable to the job for which you are applying. In this case, it may prove to be to your advantage to mention any volunteer work you did, or organizations you belonged to, as long as it does not identify your ethnicity, religious, or political affiliation (See Tip #7).

If the only job you've ever had was delivering newspapers, quantify and magnify those skills so the reader will recognize the value of your work. For example, "Distributed more than 300 journals daily to customers in assigned region," and, "Achieved a consistent 3-year 98% customer satisfaction rating," and, "Managed distribution schedule and process, resulting in a 100% on-time record."

By learning how to be creative you can draw interest to your duties without being untruthful. And that is the whole purpose of your résumé...to draw attention.

Tip #18
Lights, Camera, Action!

Use colorful action verbs to describe your duties and accomplishments. Words such as "Directed", "Integrated", "Implemented", and "Organized" will catch the attention of the recruiter or manager. Make sure you use each action word only once on your résumé. Use a thesaurus, if necessary, to find different words that mean the same thing you are trying to say.

Tip #19
99 Bottles Of Beer.

Quantify as many of your accomplishments as you can by using numbers instead of words. For example, instead of saying "Processed customer invoices", say "Pre-approved and coded in excess of $2 million in client invoices per month." It shows that you used judgment in your position, and the numbers stand out among words on your résumé. It also gives the employer an idea of the volume of work you are accustomed to dealing with relative to their needs.

Tip #20
How High Did You Go?

If you did not attend college, list the name of your high school and indicate that you received your diploma. Do not put your graduation year on your résumé unless you graduated relatively recently. Including your graduation year will reveal your approximate age and could have an adverse impact during the recruiting process (See Tip #8). It is also a good idea to list certifications as that will help give credence to your knowledge and experience.

If you earned a GED or similar certificate, list the name of the school and indicate "diploma", just as you would had you graduated from high school. There is no need to indicate that you received something other than a diploma. The idea is that you have a full and complete high school education and experience.

Tip #21
School Daze!

If you are currently attending a college or university, begin the entry with the name of the school and the year you began your education to present. For example:

University of State	2011 – Present
Biological Sciences	
Anytown High School	2011
Diploma	

This will indicate that you are currently pursuing your degree. If you have chosen a major, you may list that under the name of the school. If you have not yet completed your degree, keep your high school education on your résumé below your current college or university experience (See Tip #20).

Tip #22
Congradu'ations!

If you have completed your college or university degree program and have graduated, your education section should exclude your high school information entirely. List your college or university experience beginning with the name of your degree and the graduation year. Under the degree, you should indicate the name of the institution:

Bachelor of Science, Biological Sciences	2012
University of State	

If you have completed one degree and are currently working on another, fist of all, congratulations! On your résumé list your current degree program first followed by your completed degree. Be sure to list the school first and then major for uncompleted degrees, and degree first and then school for completed degrees (See Tip #21):

University of Other State	2013 - Present
Healthcare Informatics	
Bachelor of Science, Biological Sciences	2012
University of State	

Tip #23
For All You Know!

Your résumé should list any specific competencies you may possess. List the names of any software programs you have used or any special skills, certificates, or licenses you have acquired. Include the name of the granting institution, the certificate or license number, and the expiration date, if applicable. Make sure any licenses or certifications you include on your résumé are relevant to the job for which you are applying. If your certification has expired, don't dismiss it. It is still something you have accomplished and it should be noted. In this case, mention the certificate and remove the reference to any dates. If, and only if they ask you about your certification dates should you mention that it has expired. An exception to this would be practitioner certificates, such as nursing or technology, which are required to be current in order to practice.

Tip #24
What The Font?!

Limit your font use to 2 at the most and use **bold** and CAPS to separate sections. For easier reading, use a serif typeface (one with points at the ends of the letters), such as Times New Roman or Palatino for longer sentences. Sans-serif fonts (without serifs, or points), such as Arial or Verdana, are ok for headings and your contact information. Unless you are applying for a creative or artistic position, do not use ornate or decorative fonts! Font size should always be between 10 and 12 pts.

Under 10 pts. would be too difficult for some readers to see, and over 12 pts. would look immature and gaudy.

Tip #25
It's Not A Novel!

Keep your résumé as brief as possible while still conveying all pertinent and relevant information. For new job seekers, a one-page résumé will almost always be sufficient. If you are a seasoned employee and/or have academic credentials or more senior positions, two pages is fine. A regular job résumé should not exceed two pages.

An academic Curriculum Vitae (CV) is usually an exception to this rule, as they generally include an extensive list of publications, articles, and professional affiliations and association.

Tip #26
Paging Candidate 'X'!

If your résumé is more than one page, make sure to include your contact information (name, telephone number, email address) on the second page. It does not need to be formatted the same as the first page, but make sure it's visible. This is to ensure the employer can figure out who you are should your résumé pages become separated.

Tip #27
Form = Function!

Your résumé should be easy to read, should flow nicely, and be visually appealing. Avoid being wordy or trying to cram too much information. Short sentences and bullet points are best for most résumés. Keep in mind that most recruiters and managers take only seconds to decide whether or not to contact a job-seeker when reviewing a résumé.

Use a font size that is comfortable to the eye (See Tip #24) and use line spacing to put more white space on your résumé. White space makes individual words easier to identify, and since the potential employer will be visually scanning your résumé, looking for key words, you want to make sure those words aren't hidden amongst the other words on the page.

Tip #28
OK Captain Obvious!

Do not include the obvious on your résumé, such as "References available upon request." Employers will assume that you are able to provide references if they are requested. Such statements can make an employer think you have not done your research on résumé preparation which could hurt you in the long run.

If you have held similar positions, do not duplicate similar duties for different jobs. Each job on your résumé should show career growth and progression by showcasing unique and increasingly responsible duties and accomplishments. Redundancy will not work to your advantage.

Tip #29
I Need Proof!

Nothing screams "inattentive to detail" more than a résumé that has spelling, grammar, and typographical errors, and this is probably the one single thing that will always disqualify your résumé. Proofread your résumé 10 times. Then let 10 people proofread it 10 times each. You want to make sure you present yourself in the best possible light.

Spell-check the spell-checker. Word processing spell-checkers can't distinguish whether you want to say "Read books four children," or "Red books for children." Although the words are all spelled correctly, both sentences are grammatically incorrect. A grammar checker will identify such errors, but since your résumé is not written in prose almost every sentence will be grammatically incorrect.

In addition to proof-reading the words on your page, make sure the formatting is consistent. Your bullets should be same size and your tabs should be consistent. Make sure the heading fonts match in style and size, and the sentence fonts match in style and size. Make sure your spacing is consistent throughout. If you choose to use periods after your bullet point statements, make sure every bullet point statement has a period. Consistency is the key for a nicely formatted résumé.

Tip #30
Reach Out And Touch.

You would probably be shocked how many people carefully proofread their résumé body, and are confident that it has impeccable formatting and is error free, but neglect to make sure their telephone number and email address are correct. Review this information carefully, and verify its accuracy. Otherwise, employers won't be able to reach you.

When you are actively seeking employment, do not allow your phone to become disconnected or change your number. This is a sure way to miss out on a job. Also, make sure you turn off any blocking feature for unfamiliar numbers.

Do not include your home address on your résumé. Employers don't need to know where you live at this point, and in highly segregated cities, your address can provide a clue as to your ethnicity.

Tip #31
Do You Text?

Once your résumé is completed, proofread, and finalized, save it in a plain text format (.txt), excluding tabs, bullets, and other formatting. This will make your résumé easier to copy and paste into an email or an online ATS. Plain text résumés also "parse" much easier (See Tip #58).

Tip #32
I've Got What You Need

A cover letter is used to sell your skills and abilities. Think of your cover letter as the 30-second TV trailer and your résumé as the epic premiere. Deciding what to include in your cover letter can be tricky, but you don't want to simply reiterate what's already in your résumé. Here is a good starting point: using the job description, identify what they are looking for and provide specific examples of how you solved a problem or addressed an issue. For example:

> **Job Description –**
> Seeking a candidate with advanced PowerPoint and Excel skills.

> **Your Cover Letter –**
> Using OLE technology, I created dynamic PowerPoint presentations which linked directly to sales data in an Excel summary spreadsheet. As the sales data changed, the PowerPoint was automatically updated providing up-to-the-hour accurate information.

Since the tone of your cover letter is conversational, it is OK to use pronouns (See Tip #33).

Tip #33
Let It All Hang Out!

The cover letter is the place where you let more of your personality show in your writing. Refrain from using stodgy, formal writing, and use more conversational language. This allows the reader feel as though they are actually speaking with you face-to-face rather than just reading words about you on a sheet of paper.

The cover letter is also an appropriate place to indicate relocation preferences and desired start date. You may also mention salary expectations if, and only if the employer specifically requests it. Do not include this information if it is not explicitly requested with a phrase similar to, "Cover letters without salary expectations will not be considered."

Tip #34

3, 2, 1, Contact!

It may seem like a no-brainer, but make sure you put your complete contact information on your cover letter. You can format it to match your résumé, but this is not required. Just make sure it's on there.

Like your résumé second page, should your cover letter become separated from your résumé, you want to make sure the employer knows who you are and has a way to contact you.

Tip #35
I'm A Little Concerned!

Do not address your cover letter or email "to whom it may concern" or "Dear Sir/Madam". Do your research. Use the company website or directory to find the hiring manager's name, or look the company and position up on LinkedIn®. Be assertive. If you find someone on LinkedIn® who works for the company, ask them if they know the hiring manager's name. Most people are glad to share information. If you absolutely cannot find that person's name, simply begin your email or cover letter without a greeting.

Know someone at the company where you are applying? Drop their name in your cover letter. People, in general, like to feel a sense of connection. So if they read a cover letter and see that you have something (or someone) in common, it will grab their attention! Make sure you refer to the employee by their formal name. For example:

> I learned of this job opening from Judy Jones in Information Systems. Her glowing comments about the company inspired me to apply for the position and be a part of something great.

WARNING: If you choose to mention an employee in your cover letter, make sure the employee is in good standing within the organization.

Tip #37
The Right Key!

Many employers use an ATS to filter and organize applicant information by utilizing keywords. If your résumé says "software applications" and the keyword filter chosen is "software programs", your résumé may be skipped. Modify your résumé words and phrases to precisely match the the ones job description for best matching results.

How do you know if a company is using an ATS? If you are prompted to fill out an online application or to upload your résumé and the information "parses" into fields, chances are that you are very likely being routed through an ATS.

Tip #38
Where Are You Going?

Sometimes the best jobs may not be in your immediate area. Relocating to an area where jobs in your industry are more plentiful is an option. Research the trends in your chosen field and find out where jobs are in high demand. For example, government jobs in Washington DC, banking jobs in New York City, technical jobs in Seattle, Washington, or manufacturing jobs in Detroit, Michigan. Ok, maybe not Detroit, Michigan.

Tip #39
Déjà Vu!

If you are considering relocating for a job, try to choose an area where you can show your potential employer you have some sort of connection. For example, in your cover letter mention it if you have lived there before or if you have family currently living there. You will present yourself as a less likely flight risk should things not work out the way you expected.

Although you should not include your home address on your résumé (see Tip #30), your phone number might indicate that you are not a local candidate. Google Voice® might be a way to assign a local number to your phone to increase your chances of getting at least a phone interview.

Tip #40
Sneak Preview!

Before choosing an area for relocation, it would be a good idea to visit the area first to familiarize yourself with services, housing, and amenities. Are the social and entertainment options to your liking? Are the schools up to your standards? Are the size of the city and demographics of the area something with which you will be comfortable? Is the weather what you are looking for? All these things can be game changers in the long run, so choose carefully.

Your new job is only 1/3 of your total day, so make sure you don't accept a job just because the pay and benefits are attractive. What good is having a great job when you have no friends or family with whom to enjoy your down time, or if the climate of the area prevents you from doing things you enjoy?

Tip #41
Price Check, Please?

Make sure you consider cost-of-living differences between your current location and your desired location. An annual salary of $45K may afford you a comfortable lifestyle in Madison, Wisconsin but it may be more difficult to live a similar lifestyle in New York City or San Francisco.

Research the sales tax rates, gasoline prices, housing costs, etc. You may find that you cannot afford to live in your new city on the same salary. Keep this in mind when considering salary expectations.

Tip #42
Right On Target!

Two job search methods are often used with varying degrees of effectiveness. A broadband approach is a search for any job for which you are qualified, for example, searching for any position at any company in any location that only requires a high school diploma. A targeted approach pinpoints a specific job title in a specific industry, for example, a Finance Analyst position in a Fortune 500 company in Downtown Chicago. The more targeted your search, the less likely you will have to modify your résumé for each position for which you apply, but it will also yield fewer results in your search.

Before deciding on a search strategy, consider your work history, educational background and special training. You certainly don't want your years of experience and education to be wasted on jobs for which you are substantially overqualified, even if you are currently unemployed and just need any type of income to make ends meet.

The likelihood of an employer calling an overqualified candidate for an interview is slim. Why? Because you are a potential a flight risk. Employers realize if they hire you that you are likely to continue seeking more suitable employment and will leave as soon as a better opportunity comes along. To avoid the cost of on-boarding and training, employers only entertain candidates who are sufficiently qualified.

Tip #43
Where.com!

Internet job boards are a great way to see what types of jobs are available and which companies are posting positions. Some of the more popular job boards include: Careerbuilder.com®, Monster.com®, Indeed.com®, Hotjobs.com®, [City]jobs.com, Talentexchange.com® and Ziprecruiter.com®. There are also job boards for specific industries, such as Hcareers.com® which lists only hospitality oriented positions.

LinkedIn.com®, in addition to its professional networking features has gradually evolved into a job board. The benefits to using LinkedIn are the ability to apply instantly using your LinkedIn profile, and direct connection to the hiring managers and colleagues.

Tip #44
The Strongest Link!

LinkedIn® is a valuable resource for job seekers, even if you do not use it to specifically look for positions. Joining industry or professional groups and forums is a good way to get your name recognized, get people to look at your résumé, and possibly get referred for an excellent opportunity.

To get the most benefit from LinkedIn®, you should become an active participant in group discussions and forums. Showcase your knowledge and expertise by responding to questions. For the more advanced professional, consider doing a white paper or a blog about your industry, field, or profession and invite your connections to participate or subscribe.

Tip #45
Out Of Site!

Another way to utilize the internet to look for jobs is to focus on companies that you want to work for and keep up with their career websites. Often, these jobs do not make it to the major job boards, so fewer people are applying for these jobs.

If you are out of work, this may not be the best strategy, because the likelihood of finding an open position matching what you are seeking is small. However, if you are currently employed and can afford to wait on that ideal position, this is a great strategy.

Tip #46
Party Over There...Not Here!

Social media sites, such as Facebook® and Twitter®, should only be used for your private social life. LinkedIn® was designed as a professional networking site and should be used accordingly.

Only consider using social media sites as part of your job search strategy, if you are 100% certain that no potentially harmful material will appear on your profile or the profiles of other people with whom you are connected.

While it's not ethical, some employers do resort to Facebook® or Twitter® searches to find out how their candidates (and current employees) behave socially. Set your social media settings to private to avoid inadvertently revealing information about yourself to a potential employer.

Tip #47
I'm Board!

While internet job boards and career sites post literally millions of jobs, do not limit yourself to these sources. In-person networking is still, by far, the best pathway to new employment.

Keep open lines of communication with with former co-workers and colleagues, and talk to friends and neighbors. They can give you a heads-up when their organization is hiring, or if they know of a company that is looking to fill a position.

If your profession or industry has local organizational chapters, become a member and attend the meetings. Volunteer to facilitate a seminar or a session. Every new person you meet is an opportunity to build your professional network. Prepare, practice and use your "elevator speech" (See Tip #48).

Tip #48
Going Up?

An "elevator speech" is a statement that is designed to recite a version of your value proposition within the time it takes to make an average elevator trip. People are always interested in what you do for a living, so be prepared to impress them with something exciting and memorable so they won't forget. For example:

"Hi, I'm John Smith. I keep the best employees employed by analyzing human resources data and identifying trends and anomolies that affect retention and productivity. I've analyzed data for projects such as engagement surveys, policy changes, process standardizations, and systems implementations."

Create it. Practice it in a mirror. Hone it to perfection until it rolls right off your tongue! Remember to follow up with one of your business cards so the person you are speaking with has something to refer to once you separate from each other.

Tip #49
Don't Ask, Just Tell!

Do not directly ask anyone if they, or someone they know, are looking to fill a position for which you have an interest. It's bad manners and shows that you do not know the etiquette of networking. Simply use your elevator speech (See Tip #48) to catch their interest. Tell people what it is that you do and how you were effective in solving a problem or saving money. If you make your elevator speech interesting, people will remember you if they ever come across someone looking to fill that type of position.

Tip #50
I've Got That!

When applying for a job, always look at the list of "required" skills and credentials. If the position requires a bachelor's degree and 10 years experience, and you have an associate's degree and 2 years experience, you are not qualified for the position, and you will be wasting your time if you apply.

Conversely, "preferred" skills are things an employer would like to have from a candidate, but are willing to train or accept transferrable skills in lieu. If the position states bachelor's degree and 5 years experience preferred, and you happen to have 10 years experience in the field with some related course work, chances are the employer may strongly consider you as a viable candidate.

5 years of working in the chosen field trumps 5 years of reading books, filling in dots on a Scantron® form, and writing papers any day. Apply with confidence.

Tip #51
But Wait, There's More!

While many employers won't immediately consider an applicant who is obviously substantially overqualified on paper, there are ways to get to the interview.

Without lying, minimize your job titles and experience so they match what appears on the job description. Consider removing your advanced degree from your résumé if it is not required, or if it is not relevant to the position for which you are applying. Try using a functional résumé rather than a chronological one to highlight relevant skills and experience.

Remember, the key is to get the interview. If you can manage that, you will have every opportunity to explain anything on your résumé, or explain why, in spite of your advanced experience, you are interested in this particular position.

Tip #52
The Wages Of Sin!

Some organizations ask you for your wage or salary requirements during the application process. Be honest about your salary expectations for the position. Do some research on a site such as Salary.com® and see what the range is for the position for which you are applying, given your location, experience level, and credentials. Only provide your salary requirements if it is requested (See Tip #33).

If you are an employed job-seeker looking to advance your career, providing your salary expectation can work in your favor. In this case, be honest about what you really want for compensation. This will eliminate being called for an interview and later finding out the salary is way too low for you to consider the position.

Tip #53
The Early Bird.

If you are resorting to online job boards, make it a habit to check them daily. Some ATSs are purposely programmed to pull only the first "x" (number of) relevant applications received for a particular position. If you apply to a job toward the end of the application window, the chances of your résumé being reviewed are minimized greatly. However, if you are a diligent job seeker this shouldn't be an issue, because you are following Tip #1 and spending no less than four hours daily on your job search.

Tip #54
Amber Alert!

Most internet job boards have an alert feature which you can use to identify specific parameters to refine your job search preferences. This will make your search more efficient by sending relevant job postings directly to your email account, eliminating the need for you to search through hundreds of jobs on multiple job boards every day. These alerts can be set up to send postings daily or weekly.

Most boards will allow you to set your preferences to notify you of jobs within a certain distance, a certain industry or profession, job postings containing certain key words, or even for specific companies.

The one caveat to this strategy is you will only get those job postings whose words match exactly, and could possibly miss out on that dream job. Consider setting up several alerts with variations of your desired job title, or even comparable titles.

Tip #55
You Passed!

When applying for jobs, most job boards and company sites will require you to create a unique user ID and password. Unfortunately, log-in requirements are different for each system. While one site may only allow a 6 character username and 8 characters for your password, another site may require your email address to be used for your username and special characters and/or numbers for your password.

It is a good idea to create a list of log-in credentials for each site. In the very likely event that you forget your log-in information, this list will save you the time of having to request a user ID reminder or a password reset, or worse, having to create another user account. Should this happen and you have to create another account, you will also have to upload an enter a new résumé or job-seeker profile.

Tip #56
Give Me More!

Many employers, especially government employers, are now requiring that you submit supplementary documentation with your résumé or application. Scan your college transcripts, professional licenses, and certifications and save them as an Adobe® Portable Document Format (.pdf). Be prepared to submit these documents as attachments if they are requested.

There are many sites that will convert your scanned or typed documents for free or for a small fee. Most desktop scanners and all-in-one machines already include the Acrobat® software necessary to create the .pdf files. So if you own one of these, you are in luck!

Some online application systems often provide a place for you to cut-and-paste your résumé and cover letter within the application software. Other systems only provide an option for you to attach documents, and still others require you to fill in or will parse your information (See Tip #58).

Make sure you follow the application instructions, but if an application process permits both attaching and pasting, do both. If they also permit filling in, do all three! Recruiters or managers in the same company who may have a preference for one method over the other will be sure to receive your résumé in whichever format s/he prefers, increasing the chances that your résumé will be reviewed and considered.

Tip #58
That's Imparsable!

Many online job application systems can "parse", or automatically pull information from your résumé, to fill in the appropriate blanks in the online application form. None of them are perfect, but as you complete online applications using the parse feature, you will quickly learn which fields transfer accurately, and which need revising after parsing.

You can minimize manual entry by making changes to your plain-text résumé until you end up with one that requires little to no manual entry after the parse function is used (See Tip #31).

Tip #59
Stay On Track!

If you are applying to multiple jobs, it is quite easy to forget the details of every job for which you apply. Keep a record of all job submissions. Indicate where you found the job (website name, newspaper, etc.), the company, title of the position, where the job is located, and the date you applied. It is also ideal to save or print a copy of the job description for future reference.

Losing control of your job search is almost as bad as not searching at all. When the employer calls for a phone interview, you certainly want to remember the job, the company, and the important details of the position. Try to be prepared for an initial phone screen at all times by memorizing the positions you've applied to, or by having that information at hand. However, if at all possible do not commit to an impromtu phone interview (See Tip #60).

Tip #60
Let's Go On A Date!

Unless you are extremely organized and consistently prepared, do not accept an impromptu phone interview.

Always establish a date and time to do a phone interview. Even though interviewers realize they called you unexpectedly, if you agree to talk about the position, you are implying that you are prepared for interview questions.

If the interviewer asks if you have time to talk about the position, politely state that you would prefer to set up a date and time when you can commit your time and attention to the interview questions as well as prepare some questions for the interviewer.

Keep in mind that there are three main types of job interviews and they each serve a different purpose and are designed to solicit different types of responses and gather different information. (See Tips #63-65).

Tip #61
Get The Facts!

Before your first phone interview, be sure to research the company. Learn about their product or service, competitors, locations, history, and mission and value statements. Show that you did your homework by asking a few questions related to something you learned or found interesting about the organization.

Do not try to impress the interviewer by reciting a bunch of facts and figures that have no relevance to the position for which you are applying. That would be analogous with turning in your math homework to your English teacher!

Google® the company and look up employees on LinkedIn®. See what current and former employees are saying about the company. That will be your best insight to the company culture and climate.

Tip #62
For Example...

To prepare for interviews, commit to memory any accomplishments you have achieved at previous jobs and how they benefited the organization. Think about any difficult situations or people you encountered in the workplace, and what you did to successfully deal with them. This will help you when answering Behavioral Interview questions (See Tip #64).

If you do not have a good memory, write this information down until it comes to you naturally during interviews. Learn to transfer behavioral skills so your responses are appropriate for the question. For example, the interviewer may ask you to describe a situation where you missed a deadline. Maybe you have always met your deadlines, but try to think of a situation where you almost failed to meet a deadline, and what you did to prevent that failure.

If you did happen to miss a deadline in your work history, be honest about it, but follow up immediately with what you learned from that mistake and what steps you took to ensure that didn't happen again.

The goal of talking about shortcomings in your work history is not to point out your failures to disqualify you as a candidate, but to understand your thought processes, and personal and professional growth by hearing how you handled the situation and what you learned from it.

Tip #63
Open Sesame!

An Open Interview is the least formal interview method where the interviewer asks questions about your previous positions. You have the most flexibility and control in this type of interview, so make sure you use it to your advantage.

Brag about your accomplishments and special projects. Try to transition from one position to the next by showing how you completed projects, improved a process, and took on increased responsibility in each new position. The interviewer will likely formulate questions on the fly based on what you say about your previous work experience.

Unskilled or inexperienced interviewers will often resort to this type of interview as it only highlights your particular skills and experience. The results of the open interview are subjective as there is nothing consistent upon which candidates can be compared.

Tip #64
Ain't Misbehavin'!

A Behavioral Interview is designed to get responses describing specific examples of work-related experiences. The purpose of this type of interview is to get an idea of how you would "behave" given certain scenarios. You lose a bit of control in this type of interview because you are responding to prepared experiential questions. The results of this type of interview are more objective as an interviewer can pretty accurately gauge future performance based on past behaviors.

If you do not have the exact experience posed by the interviewer's question, be creative. Think of a work or non-work experience that presented a similar problem and resulted in a similar outcome that the interviewer is looking for (See Tip #62). Make sure you describe the steps you took to resolve the problem successfully.

Tip #65
You Need Structure!

A Structured Interview is an interview method where all candidates are asked the exact same questions in the exact same order. Organizations use this interview method to more accurately and fairly compare candidate responses, and to avoid possible future litigation or EEOC claims. Structured interviews, by their nature, ensure fairness across the candidate pool by assessing each candidate on the exact same criteria, but this type of interview also allows the least amount of latitude in interview responses.

While your responses can include specific examples, chances are the interviewer is only recording specific, qualitative information from your response. Often such characteristics such as personality, enthusiasm, and humor are excluded from the interview notes.

Tip #66
Wait, Let Me Look!

Prepare for your phone interview by reviewing your résumé and the job description beforehand. Have a copy of both in front of you during the interview so you can quickly refer to them if needed.

You should also have your list of questions for the interviewer (See Tip #70). Make sure you have enough questions written down just in case the interviewer answers some of them during the interview.

Tip #67
Believe The Skype®!

More and more, employers are arranging interviews using Skype® or some other video chat service. It is a good idea to establish a Skype® account and become familiar with its features and functions by having video chats with friends and family. This will make it much easier for you to engage in an interview using this technology should you happen to secure an interview with an organization that utilizes it. As with your email address, your Skype username should be appropriate (See Tip #9).

Should you happen to have a video interview, prepare as you would an in-person interview. Make sure your visual background is clean and free of clutter. Make sure there are no windows behind you with sunlight coming through as this will affect the quality of the video. Try to stage your surroundings: move a bookshelf or a plant into the background. Make sure any visible artwork or decorations are appropriate. You want your environment to look as much like an office as possible.

Tip #68
A Noise That Annoys!

During your phone interview, make sure you are alone in a quiet room. Turn off the television or music source and try to make sure there are no children or pets in the area that might disturb you. Avoid conducting your interview in a restaurant or coffee shop as the ambient noise and background music can obscure your responses and frustrate your interviewer.

If you live by an airport or close to an elevated train, an industrial area, or some other noise producing environment, try to find an alternative place to conduct your phone interview.

Tip #69
See No Evil!

Just because it's a phone interview does not mean you should not dress for it. Prepare for it and behave just as you would at an in-person interview. Take a shower or bath, brush your teeth, get dressed in a comfortable, business-casual outfit, put on your shoes, and do your hair. Sit upright in your chair as you would during an in-person interview.

Sound silly? You would be surprised how these small details can affect your posture, attitude, and voice during a phone interview (See Tip #85). If you are too relaxed, your responses will come across as very relaxed, and the interviewer may get the impression that you aren't taking the interview seriously.

Tip #70
Trinity & Beyond!

No, not *that* Trinity. This isn't about religion. Even during the preliminary phone interview, prepare at least 3 questions to ask your interviewer. Depending on the type of job, good questions for this stage in the interview process are: "Is this a new position, and, if not, why is it vacant?", "Is this singular role or are there others also performing this role?", "How many people are in the department?", "Is there a reason nobody was promoted to this position?", "What is the reporting structure for the department?"

Failure to ask questions may give the impression that you are either not interested, or are willing to accept any position offered to you. You want to make sure your new position is a good fit for your skills, abilities and even your personality and work style. Form your questions to get answers that speak to these issues.

Tip #71
One Moment, Please!

When answering interview questions, take a moment to pause and think about your answer before responding. If you are unclear of what is being asked, it is perfectly fine to ask the interviewer to rephrease the question or provide clarification. You want to make sure to give the "best" answer to the question being asked. Answering too quickly might make it appear that your responses are rehearsed, or that you haven't given any significant thought to what the interviewer is asking you.

If you find yourself engaged in a structured interview, you should still try to support each of your responses with a brief example from a previous position. Even though your examples may not be recorded, it will show that you completely understand the question and have put thought into your answer.

Tip #72
Don't Hang Up!

Beforing ending your phone interview, make sure you thank the interviewer for calling and wish him or her a nice day/evening/weekend! This may not seem like much, but just consider what an interviewer might think if you fail to extend that courtesy.

Remember, interviewers are humans and have feelings and emotions as well. You want to maintain as much of a feel-good connection as possible between yourself and the people with whom you speak at the organization. They will remember that.

Tip #73
Come On In!

Consider your daily activities before committing to a date and time for an in-person interview. Child-care needs, your current work schedule, transportation, etc. can all impact your availability for an interview.

The last thing you want to do is schedule an in-person interview, and then realize you have to reschedule it due to lack of planning on your part. Worst case scenario: all interview slots have been filled and you completely miss out on the opportunity.

Before beginning the interview stage of your job search, have a definite plan in place for child care, transportation and other situations that could prevent you from meeting your interview appointment.

Tip #74
Do You Copy, Copy, Copy?

When you are arranging your in-person interview, try to find out who you will be meeting. Prepare an interview folder for each person with whom you are scheduled to speak. Each folder should include a copy of your résumé, cover letter, references, and any other documents that you feel will help you sell yourself as the right candidate.

Remember, the goal during the in-person interview is to impress the interviewer, not only with your skills, but your ability to organize and present.

Tip #75
Any Questions?

Arrive at your interview with a prepared list of questions, preferably different questions than the ones you asked during your phone interview. It is perfectly OK to have them written down and to read directly from the paper.

Some questions you could ask are: "How long do employees typically stay in this position?", "Have previous employees in this position been promoted or did they leave the organization?", "What are the personal characteristics you would expect the candidate to have for this position?", "What would be the career progression from this position within this organization, if any?", "What have been some of the challenges with this position in the past?"

Tip #76
Um, Ya Know, Like, So...Yeah!

Practice responding to interview questions without using filler words and phrases. Effective, professional communication is essential, not only in an interview, but also on the job. Verbal ticks can be annoying and can make it appear that you are either not prepared, or that you are making up answers, or that you simply lack communication skills.

If you are able, record yourself during a conversation so you can hear exactly how you sound. You just may be surprised how often you use verbal ticks, slang, and unprofessional speech. It's OK to be somewhat casual in your interview, but not to the extent that you act like you are talking to your friends in a club.

Tip #77
Have A Fit!

Make sure you dress appropriately for the interview (See Tip #78). Follow any guidance offered by the manager or recruiter. But in the absence of any instruction, here is a guide: for professional and administrative positions, a suit and tie (men) or pants or skirt suit and blouse (women) would be appropriate. For service industry positions, slacks, khakis or chinos and a shirt & tie (men), or a skirt and blouse/sweater (women) is appropriate. Only wear closed toe shoes.

For labor positions, jeans are probably acceptable, but khakis or chinos, and a collared or a polo-style shirt makes a better impression.

Tip #78
Hey, Look At Me!

Avoid wearing loud colors, busy patterns or any outfit or accessories that might make you stand out for all the wrong reasons. Stick with the solid, traditional "interview" colors: black, grey, blue, and brown.

Remember, interviewers are human and, as such, have their own likes, dislikes, prejudices, preferences and favorites. You don't want to eliminate yourself before being given a fair chance because you wore something inappropriate or unattractive (See Tip #77).

Tip #79
No Access!

Along with your clothing, make sure you are also conservative with your accessories, make-up and hair. Men should trim and clean your nails and try to have a fresh haircut. Women should only wear clear or a natural-colored nail polish and go lightly on make-up. Earrings for women should be limited to studs or small hoops. For men, if you are interviewing for a professional position, earrings should be removed.

Other jewelry should be minimal: a wedding band/ring, one other ring, one bracelet, one simple necklace, and a watch. Depending on the position, make sure tattoos are covered when possible and any facial piercings are removed.

Tip #80
What's That Smell?

Avoid taking the smell of your environment with you to your interview. If at all possible, avoid cooking, smoking, and consuming aromatic foods and beverages prior to your interview. Carrying odors from your environment might make it appear that this interview is an interruption in your day and you may not be taken seriously.

Also avoid wearing perfumes or colognes or using heavily scented soaps or lotions. Some scents, while fragrant and pleasing to you, could be overpowering, offensive and/or distracting, and you could ruin your chances of being selected.

Tip #81
Can't Make It!

If you experience some unforseen circumstance on the way to the interview, call your contact and let them know what happened, and ask if you should still come in for the interview or if you should reschedule.

Keep in mind, the only thing that should alter your interview schedule should be a situation outside of your control that occurs on the way to your interview, such as a vehicle break-down, severe traffic, public transit delays, etc. Failure to secure a babysitter, waking up late, or having a flat tire are not valid excuses for not being on time, and only exposes your inability to prepare. "A flat tire?" you may ask. Yes! A flat tire or car not starting is not an excuse to be late for an interview. If you have an interview at 10:00am, go outside at 7:00 am and make sure your car starts and all tires are inflated while you still have time to correct the unforseen issue without being late.

Tip #82
What Time Is It?

Arrive for your interview at least 5 minutes before the scheduled time, but no more than 15 minutes. Arriving less than 5 minutes before will make it seem like you didn't plan your trip and rushed to your interview. More than 15 minutes might make it seem like you are in a hurry to get the interview over with.

Consider taking a test drive the day before to familiarize yourself with the trip, and to make sure you do not get lost and risk being late for the interview. Make sure to take plenty of change with you in case you have to park at a meter or pay tolls.

When you arrive let the receptionist know who you are interviewing with, and take a seat in the lobby or waiting area (See Tip #83).

Tip #83
The Lobby-ist!

Treat the receptionist as part of your interview team. This individual is also indirectly interviewing you, taking note of how you introduce yourself, how you sit, and what you do while you wait for your interview.

While waiting, review your résumé or read some of the provided literature in the reception area, especially anything related to the company. If there is artwork, framed articles, or other décor that interests you, it is OK to observe and admire it.

Texting or playing a game on your cell phone may translate as being unprofessional. By this point your phone should be off or on silent, and not simply on vibrate. Under no circumstances should you call or accept a call from from anyone. This is the time you set aside for your interview, so do not share that time with anyone else.

Tip #84
Flip/Flop!

When you arrive for your interview, greet everyone, even the receptionist, with a smile. Introduce yourself to each of your interviewers with a smile, a firm handshake, and look them directly in the eye when speaking to them.

Be confident, but not cocky. Interview like you have the ability to do the job, but not like you know more than the person interviewing you. Be humble, but not timid. Respect the authority and knowledge of the person interviewing you, even if you are more experienced and more knowledgeable. But do not allow the interviewer's authoritative position keep you from asserting your qualifications and experience. Be appreciative, but not desperate. Thank the interviewer for the opportunity to interview for the position, and make your closing request for the job. But do not demonstrate that you are in dire need of the position, even if you are. Don't ever beg for a position. Showing too much desperation can translate into you being willing to accept the first job offer that comes across your plate, which may also mean you will jump ship at the first better opportunity. Employers look for these signs when interviewing.

Tip #85
Have a Seat!

During your interview, sit upright in your chair, leaning slightly forward. Crossing your arms is a subconscious defensive posture, so avoid doing it at all costs. Instead, keep your hands folded in your lap or on the table. It is OK to use your hands to gesture as you speak. Crossing your legs is fine, even if there is no table to be a buffer between you and the interviewer.

Make sure you are comfortable in your seat before you begin. Shifting in your seat may cause the interviewer to think you are nervous about the questions. Always maintain a natural but professional demeanor and tone during your interview.

It is also OK to take notes during your interview. If you do take notes, be careful not to tap your pen on your notepad or fidget with your pen. Hold it still in your hand. If that proves to be a challenge, place the pen on your pad until you need to use it.

Tip #86
Forget Chew!

It is simply poor etiquette to chew gum or suck on mints or lozenges during your interview. If you are conscious about your breath, chew gum or suck a mint right before you go in to your interview. Throw it in the trash before you take your seat. Most interviewers will offer you a bottled water to keep your throat moist while talking. Accept the water and use it if necessary to wet your whistle.

Tip #87
Free To Be Me!

One interview tactic is to make you feel comfortable and relaxed so that you will feel more casual in sharing your work and life experiences. Always keep in mind that you are in an interview with a potential employer, not at a bar with an old friend.

Beware of any questions that may cause you to reveal something about yourself or a previous position that could be detrimental to your candidacy (See Tip #88). No matter now comfortable or confident you may feel be careful of revealing adverse information about previous employment (See Tip #89).

Tip #88
They Fought The Law...

Unless it is a Bona Fide Occupational Qualification (BFOQ), requiring answers to certain questions is illegal. However, unless you are well-versed in employment law, you may not recognize these questions right away, if at all. Questions relating to age, sexual orientation, political views, religious affiliation, disability, marital and/or family status, previous job-related injuries, medical history, military experience, and many other questions could be illegal and prohibited by Federal or State law.

No matter how comfortable you are in your interview, and no matter how friendly your interviewer seems, be careful that you do not inadvertently give responses that might provide information identifying you as belonging to a protected class.

Experienced interviewers know to avoid these types of questions, but if these types questions arise, try your best to circumvent by responding in a way that gives a neutral answer, or deflect by answering a different question entirely.

Tip #89
Nothing Nice To Say?

Do not speak negatively about a previous employer. If you left a previous employer because of a personality clash, policy, or pay, re-word it in a more positive way so as not to disparage your former employer.

For example, instead of saying, "My former boss was such a jerk," respond with, "I am seeking a position with an organization that has a more open and collaborative management style." Instead of saying, "My last job paid peanuts and I've got bills to pay," say, "I feel that my ability to learn and grow at my previous employer had peaked and it was time for me to pursue opportunities that can accommodate my potential." Of course, whatever you come up with, be able to support it with examples.

Tip #90
Show Me The Money!

Although it is obvious that the salary is an important part of a job, voicing your salary requirements too early in the selection process will make it appear that you are more interested in a paycheck than the actual opportunity itself!

Ideally, the salary will be part of the job posting. If so and you applied or submitted your résumé, that salary is acceptable to you. If it's not included with the job posting do some research to get an idea of what the salary for the position might be in the particular industry and region.

Some organizations request your salary expectations during the application process. If you provided an honest range, and you were subsequently called for an interview, the employer will more than likely offer you a salary within your requested range (See Tip #52).

Tip #91
It's Goin' Down!

You should periodically take the temperature of your interview. An unskilled interviewer will often show tell-tale signs that your interview is not going well. If your interviewer stops taking notes and puts his or her pen down that is a sign that s/he has lost interest. If the pace of the interviewing suddenly increases, or the interviewer starts looking at a watch or clock, that may be a sign that the interviewer is bored and is rushing to get through the interview. If the interviewer suddenly picks up your résumé and continues to read it while you are talking, chances are the interview is over. If your interviewer starts looking away instead of looking into your eyes, s/he probably has doubts about your truthfulness.

If you suspect the interview is on the decline, be straightforward and ask the interviewer if there is there anything you can clarify, or if there is something you said that caused the interviewer to lose interest. It will show that you are observant and that you are interested in his or her feelings or impressions. At this point you have nothing to lose and you just may just salvage your interview.

Tip #92
Pick A Card!

After you complete your interview with each person at the organization, be sure to ask them for a business card. If they do not have one, ask them for their contact information (name and email address at minimum) and write it down in your portfolio. You will want this information so you can send thank you letters or emails following your interview. This has become an expected gesture and failing to formally thank your interviewer could potentially disqualify you as a candidate.

If they are hesitant to provide this information, or you forget to ask for a card, do not despair. If you have a first and last name, and at least one other person's email address, then you can probably figure out everyone else's email based on the email formatting convention the organization uses.

For example, if you interviewed and received a business card from John Jones and his email address is "jjones@company.com", and you interviewed with Richard Smith but didn't get his card, it is safe to assume his email address is "rsmith@company.com".

Tip #93
The Secret Code!

Some organizations maintain a dress code that may or may not be documented and specifically outlined. If so, it will very likely be covered in the new employee orientation. But while you are there for your interview, take a mental note of what employees in positions similar to yours are wearing. If it happens to be a Friday and people are wearing jeans, ask if it's Casual Friday. An affirmative response will indicate that there is a designated dress code.

You should prepare to mirror what you see as the prevailing apparel. You do not want to come to your first day of work over-dressed or under-dressed. If it is not apparent or mentioned, it's a safe assumption that the attire is business casual for most office positions.

Tip #94
Watch Your Back!

Your interview does not end when you leave the interviewer's office or the conference room. Remain professional as you leave, extending salutations to the receptionist. Speak to those you encounter on your way out of the building because you never know who they are and how they might be connected to the department or the people in the department in which you just interviewed.

Only when you have reached the comfort of your own vehicle, or taxi, or bus, or train, or bicycle should you allow yourself to unwind and let your guard down. Only then should you check emails, texts, voice mails, and call your best friend to let him know how the interview went.

Tip #95
Thanks For Everything!

As soon as you are able, but definitely within 24 hours, send a thank you email to every person with whom you interviewed. Some people prefer to send thank you letters, but by the time your letter reaches the interviewer, everyone else's thank-you emails have been read, and quite possibly the candidate pool narrowed. If you for some reason think a letter will make a better impression, then go ahead and send it.

In your letter or email enthusiastically recap some of the most important points you talked about during the interview and remind them why you are the best candidate for the position. Again, ask for the job, but do not beg (See Tip #84).

Send a separate email or letter to each person rather than CCing several people in a single email or letter. If you are sending emails and don't have an email address for each person, simply use the apparent email convention to send emails to everyone (See Tip #92). Address each person by name.

Tip #96
Would You Like Seconds?

Congratulations, you've made it to the second round of interviews! At this point the employer has already determined that you are qualified to do the job. Some of your competition has been eliminated and they are probably down to the top candidates, usually between 2 and 5 people. Second interviews are generally designed to see whether you are a fit for the company and the department. During the second interview, you may meet with other people in the department or from other departments.

Pay close attention to the personalities of the people you speak with and mirror their dispositions. If the person interviewing you is casual, be cautiously casual. If they are more formal, mirror their formal demeanor. However, do not portray a false personality that you can't consistently live up to. If you do, you may find yourself working with people that you really don't get along with.

Try to wear a different outfit than you did at your first interview so you appear fresh and different. You still want to make sure your attire is appropriate for an interview (See Tip #77-79), and that you maintain your professional and enthusiastic demeanor (See Tip #83-89).

Tip #97
Flip The Script

A second interview is also your opportunity for you to interview your interviewer. Try to prepare questions for each person with whom you may come in contact. Focus your questions on job interactions and express particular interest in each person's role in the organization. Think about scenarios that you have faced on previous jobs, or that you anticipate having in this position, and form your questions to see how the manager or colleague would respond in situations.

Questions such as, "How long have you been in your current role?", "What are some of the challenges you face in your role?", "How does this role interact with others in the department/in other departments?" are all appropriate questions for this interview stage.

You should ask questions about the company culture, organizational structure, and the strategic importance of the department within the organization. Look for answers to these questions on the organization's website, and ask the interviewer how they personally feel about what the website says. This will show that you are being selective about joining the organization.

Tip #98
Watch Your Step!

It is acceptable to ask about next steps in the selection process if the interviewer does not automatically offer this information to you. You may want to ask how many candidates remain at this point, when they expect the interview period to end, and when they expect to make a decision. This will give you an idea of whether or not you have been selected after that time period has passed, and it will also give you an idea of how many candidates they are considering.

Tip #99
Follow The Leader!

If you really want the job for which you interviewed, it is fine to contact the hiring manager or recruiter to keep your name in their minds during the selection process. When interviewers tell you after an interview, "If you have any questions in the meantime feel free to give me a call or send me an email," this is your invitation to keep in contact, reiterating your desire and fit for the position. Do not make more than two phone calls or email contacts per week.

A good way to sedgeway into an email is to follow the organization on Twitter® or keep up with any media reports about the organization or industry (good or bad). Send an email referencing the article or Tweet® and ask a question about it. For example, you may come across an article about the company doing an acquisition or a merger. Copy the article link and ask a brief question. For example:

Dear [Manager]:

I came across this article and I was wondering if this acquisition will have any direct effect on processes in the Finance department. I would be interested in hearing your views on this:

http://www.article.com/583ud8e

Thank you for reading!

This will show that you are interested in the company and are thinking strategically.

Tip #100
Either Way!

"You will hear from us either way," does not always necessarily mean you will hear from them at all. Make a note of the date they expect to fill the position. If you have not heard anything from the company by that date, it is ok to contact them and ask about the status of the position. If they inform you that the position has been filled, politely say "Thank you." Follow up with an email thanking the manager for the opportunity to interview and express that you would like to be considered for other positions within the organization.

Should the selected candidate subsequently decline the offer, or maybe doesn't pass a drug or background check, or maybe even decides it isn't the right position, you want to make sure the manager remembers you. Rather than go through the entire recruiting process again, employers generally contact the runner up. Keep in mind, you won't know that you're the runner up candidate unless you receive a rejection letter prior to being reconsidered for the position.

But hopefully, your phone is about to ring, and you will soon be receiving that verbal job offer! Bask in your success and take some time to celebrate!

Tip #101
Start Over!

Now that you have that dream job, you can forget everything you've learned, file away that résumé, throw out that jos site password list and take it easy, right? Wrong! This is the ideal time to reflect on things you did right and things you did wrong in your job search. This will probably not be the last time you have to go through this process so you want to make sure you are prepared the next time you are in the market for a new or better job.

Keep your working résumé up to date by constantly adding the new skills, experiences and projects from your new job. By doing this as you learn and grow in your new job, you won't have to try to remember everything you have learned over the years.

Remember to also update all the online profiles and job boards with your new position and skills. Do it gradually just in case your current employer is following your profile. Entering all your new skills at one time may signal you are job-seeking.

Continue to network with people from previous employers, recruiters, and people you have met along your job search journey. You never know when you may need them again, and they may remember you when that even better opportunity comes up!

For complementary resume review

or questions, please email:

info@westone-management.com

For more specific career counseling, visit:

www.westone-management.com/contact